INTRODUCTION

THE STUDY OF PLANTS

Maurice Pillard Verneuil
Extract from L'Etude de la plante et ses applications aux industries d'art.
[1908]

Among the various elements called into play when an ornamental work is produced, the plant is certainly the one which displays the widest variety in its forms and best lends itself to decorative combinations. In a word, the plant is the most resourceful element at our disposal.

Furthermore, the briefest survey of ornamental art through the ages should be enough to convince us that the plant has long been used as a feature in decorative art.

But it was during the Middle Ages in particular that the use of plants was of great importance, and a direct study of nature in its most humble aspects was to inspire the sculptors of our cathedrals to achieve decorative splendour incomparable in its richness and originality. From the essence of parsley, cress, ferns and a thousand other common plants, they could extract capitals and friezes with a beauty of line, a boldness and a sureness of interpretation that surprise and captivate us. Breaking away from the example of their immediate predecessors, they returned to that eternal source of inspiration, nature, where they were to find an inexhaustible supply of beauty on which to draw. An awareness of the craftsmanship that would be called upon to realize their decorative projects led them to conceive their designs with a clear, rational

DECORATIVE FLOWERS

DECORATIVE FLOWERS

after the plates by
M. P. Verneuil

selection and commentary by
William Wheeler

Michael O'Mara Books Limited

First published in Great Britain in 1998 by
Michael O'Mara Books Limited
9 Lion Yard
Tremadoc Road
London SW4 7NQ

The texts of the Introduction and Ornamental Grounds in the
Appendices are extracts from *L'Etude de la plante et ses applications aux
industries d'art* by Maurice Pillard Verneuil, first published in 1908.

Acknowledgements
We would like to thank the Bibliothèque des Arts Décoratifs in Paris
and its chief curator, Madame Bonté, for her invaluable help with this
project.

A CIP catalogue record for this book is available from the British
Library

ISBN 1-85479-293-8

1 3 5 7 9 10 8 6 4 2

Typeset by K DESIGN, Winscombe, Somerset
Printed and bound in Italy

TABLE OF CONTENTS

FOREWORD

Maurice Pillard Verneuil published *L'Etude de la plante et ses applications aux industries d'art (The Study of the Plant and its Applications in Art Industries)* when he was nearly forty years old. He was born in 1869 in France at Saint Quentin dans l'Aisne, and received his artistic education in the grand tradition of figurative painting, in which the acquisition of a properly grounded technique was paramount. Those who used their talents for decorative purposes were destined for low-prestige careers, yet it was in the vast area of the applied arts that Verneuil chose to exercise his skills. His meeting with Eugène Grasset [1841–1917] was to be decisive. It was Grasset who was to elevate the rank of decorative artists in France, in much the same way as William Morris [1834–1917] had in England. The impact of japonisme on Grasset's style is matched by the influence of the highly stylized plant forms which would make Art Nouveau aesthetics universally identifiable. As one of Grasset's students, Verneuil was encouraged to work along similar lines. Indeed, thanks to Eugène Grasset, a whole generation of young designers were brought together. As one of the most gifted among them, Verneuil, along with Auguste Giacometti, brother of the sculptor, was invited by Grasset to work on his major publication, *La Plante et ses applications ornementales* [1897]. It was during the time Verneuil was associated with this project that he began to establish his own personal style of expression. He became very interested in stencilling. By means of this very simple process – cutting holes in a piece of card or metal and brushing colour through them onto paper underneath – Verneuil was able to create elegant decorative effects. Numerous examples will be shown here to illustrate his talent with this technique. Following his teacher's example, Verneuil published several of his own studies, most notably: *L'Animal dans la décoration, Combinaisons ornementales se multipliant à l'infini à l'aide du miroir*, which was produced in collaboration with Georges Auriol and Alphonse Mucha, *L'Ornementation par le pochoir, Etoffes japonaises tissées et brochées* and *Etudes de la mer. L'Etude de la plante et ses applications aux industries d'art* is a direct tribute to Eugène Grasset, even though in this work one can see how the pupil had by now found his own personal voice.

Like many decorative artists, Verneuil worked on posters, but it was not a field in which his style succeeded. He was also the author of a curious dictionary called *Dictionnaire des symboles, emblèmes et attributs*, in which he combined familiar references with other more esoteric ideas that resulted from his own research. His last important publication was *Kaléidoscope*, in which he adopted the prevalent style of the 1920s, Art Deco. He died in 1942.

approach. They had, in effect, both knowledge of and respect for the two laws that preside over any good ornamental project: a thorough understanding both of the source of inspiration for the design and of the techniques of the craft that would be used to execute it. Not enough attention is paid to these two preoccupations nowadays.

Designers imagine that they can somehow create perfectly conceived ornamental work instinctively without research. But this creative process is not as easy as it seems. This means that a well-founded work demands a knowledge both of the principal laws of ornamental art and of the complete techniques of the craft used to execute it. For ornamentation to be beautiful, it must not only be a pleasant, well-balanced composition but attention must be paid to the materials used, for they will add their own distinctive character.

Constant repetition and slavish imitation of former styles forestalls originality of conception. Henceforward, a return to nature is imperative and consequently a complete study of it becomes indispensable.

THE INTERPRETATION OF PLANTS

A serious question in the field of ornamental art is posed by the act of interpretation. Two rules are absolute, and if they are ignored, no rational decoration can exist. They apply to the adaption of the design to fit the space to be decorated, and to the adaptation of that space according to the materials used.

These two important principles, the two bases of decorative art, must always be foremost in our minds when we embark on a composition. And if observing these rules occasionally makes work on the conception rather laborious, it is none the less the rules which confer style, the prerequisite of all ornamental work.

In adapting the form to the space to be decorated, we shall concentrate on the balance of the different blocks and the theme of the composition in relation to

Border.

13

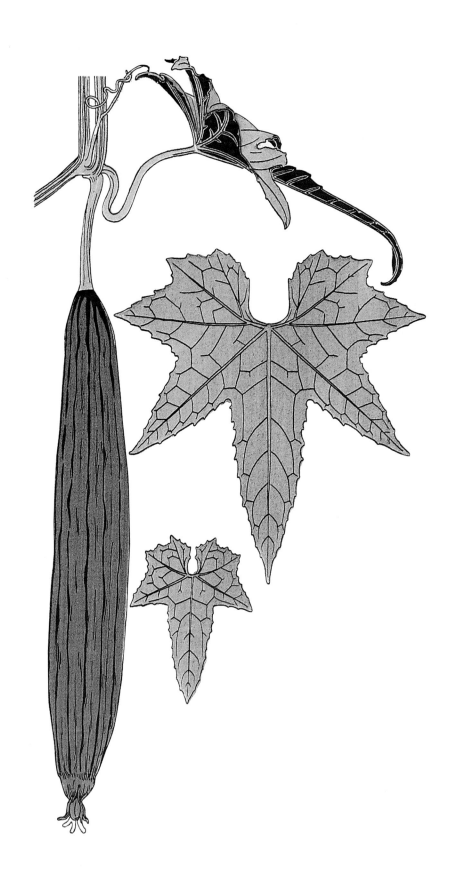

*Towel gourd. Details of the
fruit and the leaf.*

*Opposite: Woven fabric with
straight repeat.*

a specific effect. In each case, the motifs are arranged, the patterns are grouped or spaced. One part of the plant is lengthened, another is shortened. A rigid stem is made supple, a corner which would otherwise remain empty is embellished.

But what about the theme of a composition? It is the layout, the arrangement of the decorative elements that dictate it, often a plan which has as its goal a reasoned and coherent effect. For ornamentation is not only loading or overloading an object with decoration. It is important that the decorative elements be intelligently planned for several reasons: to honour the materials used, to emphasize the particular characteristic of the subject matter, and to ensure the decorative motif used will harmonize with the form it will cover.

In several of the examples we have intentionally covered all the free space on the imposed surface. And once again, for one of the reasons cited above, we can put limits on a form of ornamentation when it comes to decorating a different space or object. Hence, in this rectangular bookcover decorated with typographical ornamentation, a cartouche containing the embellished first letter of the title has to be carefully arranged. These are only two examples picked from a thousand others.

We have already observed the importance of the balance between different blocks. From the outset we must foresee the overall effect the composition will produce once it is finished. We must arrange the solid and hollow elements, as we do the light and dark ones, to guarantee the homogeneity and the complete balance of the composition.

Finally, the decoration takes on its own character, depending on whether it is to be used to embellish a monument or a room.

The technical requirements of the craft to be used to execute our composition will settle all the details concerning the adaptation of the form to the materials used. For, to make an attractive design, it is crucial that the drawings can be executed with ease, so that there are no occasions on which the manufacturer finds himself obliged to perform hazardous feats which can only lead to two conclusions: the labour costs rising and a complete lack of style in the object produced. In a word, why ask a craft to do that which it is incapable of doing?

Why dissimulate the process when it is precisely this that gives character to the work? The craftsman has to be able to give full rein to his professional capacities and set off the materials to best effect. Why scrape and polish sculpted wood to conceal every trace of the chisel and give it the unattractive aspect of a walnut-stained moulding? Why file down and smooth wrought iron to erase the marks of the hammer and make it resemble a cast piece? Why should we want a printed fabric to look exactly like a woven fabric? Surely it is better to illuminate the particular beauty of each craft. Let it be obvious that wood is hewn and that iron is wrought. Both can only gain in character.

Thus, one of the essential preconditions of carrying out work of value in any one branch of the decorative arts is a depth of knowledge of the techniques used and respect, not only for the materials, but also for the craftsmanship involved. It is essential to reject all forms and formulas that are not feasible. As we have said, with this rule of thumb, the interpretative element of a project can be realized: in a word, its style.

So, what is interpretation? Interpretation is the simplification, the ornamentation of a form passing from its natural state to an ornamental state. In effect, by disregarding the picturesque in a plant or a flower, we extract and create an ornamental principle.

In our initial study of plants, we should already have made every effort to simplify and schematize: this is the beginning of interpretation. We have sought to inscribe each form within a geometrical figure. The transposition of the natural form into geometrical ones is stylization at its simplest.

Thus, if we wish to interpret a plant for decorative purposes (while complying with the established rules), we must first take account of the various elements that our study has revealed. By simplifying and reorganizing them, we reconstitute an ornamental form in compliance with the necessary requirements of a valid, easily executed decoration.

Two main ideas should guide us in our interpretation: the beauty inherent in the form and the ease with which it can be realized using one's chosen materials. Each new industry will dictate a new manner of interpretation. A rough material like iron will require significant simplifications; lace, however, calls for finesse and detail. But always, and in every case, the rule of the plant itself

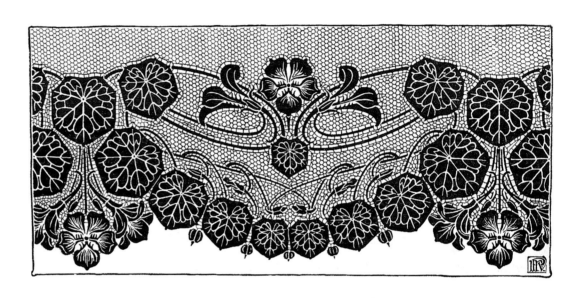

Top:
Nasturtium. Border.
Bottom:
Branche-ursine. Fan.

Brambles. Wrought-iron fence.

What do we mean by a colour scale? It is a series of different values intended to create a harmony. And by the different colour values, I don't mean you to think that the colours must be different, but rather their values or tones. For a monochrome can give rise to such a scale, even when there is only one colour, because there will still be grades of intensity.

This leads us to defining a colour's value. Value is the amount of light and dark that enters into the composition of a tone.

As we have already mentioned, a scale is a series of coloured values. In creating the scale, our intention is to establish the value of our subject. This is the most important aspect of the subject of colour: the application of values.

The effect depends on this and this alone. A single example can make the point. By using the same colour in differing values, a huge variety of effects can be created. A monochrome can quite easily give the impression of the sun if the relationship between the values or tones is correct. It could just as well give the impression of night. The most brilliant or the darkest of colours will not produce this effect if the relationship between the colour's values is not properly regulated.

It is self-evident that a motif will not stand out against a background of the same value. We have to concern ourselves with an equilibrium of values, just as we had to face similar concerns with mass and line. We should also be occupied by the influence of values on one another.

From top to bottom:
Bindweed. Single-colour stencil.
Oleander. Border.
Castor-oil plant. Border.
Pomegranate. Mosaic frieze.

23

MAJESTIC BULBS

IRIS

Maurice Pillard Verneuil held the decorative potential of the iris in high esteem. Hence, it is not at all surprising that its importance in *L'Etude de la plante* is equal to that of the lily. According to some historians, the iris, which is often the garden and symbolical rival of the lily, actually inspired the trilobate sign, the fleur-de-lis. If one observes the flower in profile, especially the yellow flag iris, which is indigenous to marshes, the symmetry of the erect petals does bring to mind the heraldic emblem.

None the less, the artist's preference was for the German iris, also called the bearded iris, a standard in gardens of all sizes. When Charles Linnaeus established his binomial nomenclature during the seventeenth century, the classification system still used today, several errors crept into the iris section, which included about twenty different species, including the *Iris germanica*. The specimen plant he used for his research had been sent to him from a German garden, although it was not indigenous to that country. This

German iris

Opposite:
German iris. Wallpaper frieze.

taxonomic detail did nothing to deter Verneuil from implementing designs of it in materials as different as lace and ironwork. Even on the delicate lace shawl, the character of the bearded iris combines the masculine and the feminine: the strength of the large, stocky, spear-shaped sepals encircle the elegant, sensuous curves of the flower.

The complexity of the flower allows Verneuil to give full rein to his imagination in a series of diversified projects. Very discreet in the botanical study, the 'beard' adorning the petals is exaggerated in the projects to such an extent that it becomes an over-sized motif in itself. Whether it be for the lace shawl, the iron fence coping, the wallpaper border, or even the carved wood frieze, the flower design is very similar. It expresses massiveness while emphasizing the torsional strain of the petals. In fact, Verneuil showed exactly how he arrived at this interpretation through a series of six models, six variations on the same theme. The petals are transformed into basic geometrical figures: circle, square, rhombus, semi-circle, triangle (joined at the base or the apex). Unfortunately, the artist did not utilize them per se in his projects. Based on a circular design, the iris figured on the stained glass with its long, swaying blades is more delicate, lighter, as if the flowers were slowly rocking in an aquatic setting. Their erect, yellow petals form handsome fleurs-de-lis.

German iris. Various geometrical interpretations of the flower.

Top :
German iris. Carved wood
frieze.
Bottom:
German iris. Wrought-iron
fence coping.

29

German iris. Stencilled border and sprig pattern.

30

German iris. Leaded-glass window.

Following pages: Iris. Coloured glass window.

German iris. Lace shawl.

34

Iris. Decorated ground.

35

EASTER LILY

Easter lily. The whole plant and a detail of the flower.

Opposite:
Easter lily. Decorative border.

The emblematic flower *par excellence*, this white lily, *Lilium candidum*, is the best-known member of this prestigious family. Since antiquity, it has beguiled by its beauty and abundant blooming. For thousands of years it has been cultivated in royal gardens because lords and kings saw in it a symbol of their power and used it to manifest their influence. As the symbol of the Virgin Mary as well as of the French monarchy, this eminent flower seems to demand a treatment faithful to nature. Perhaps as a consequence of either too much respect or too little interest, Verneuil's botanical study of the flower is irreproachable, but lacks sincerity. Content with portraying the lily in all its immaculate splendour, he added none of his accustomed fanciful touches. The presentation is classical and conventional, not far from that of Redouté, a century earlier. Whether he emphasized the symmetry of the individual flower structure or the asymmetry of their arrangement on the graceful stalk, Verneuil's handling of this plant shows cold, clinical precision.

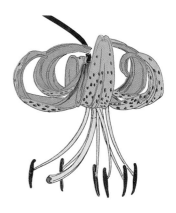

TIGER LILY

There is no doubt that the colour of the Easter lily and its religious and royalist connotations did little to inspire Verneuil. However, several other types of lily seem to have been more to his liking. Of Chinese origin, the tiger lily was cultivated there for centuries before being introduced into Europe at the turn of the nineteenth century. Its culture is almost as ancient as that of *Lilium candidum*. In the botanical study, to accentuate its elegance, the artist painted a stalk stripped of many of its numerous flowers and leaves. He even drew a lone pistil which has completely shed its withered petals. Through a similar process of simplification, Verneuil proceeded in like fashion to Pierre-Joseph Redouté who, in his major work, *Les Liliacées*, painted the tiger lily with a single, mature flower at the top of the stalk. Verneuil gracefully arranged the various details of the flower on the page in pairs, thus proving that he granted as much importance to the page layout as to the flower itself. The projects, a woven fabric and a stamped, gold-plated plaque, both play on a side view of the plant. The treatment of the foliage, especially on the plaque, is reminiscent of that used for acanthus leaves by the Greeks and the Romans. Verneuil accentuated the curled petals, turbanesque, without overlooking aspects of the elongated, swollen flower buds. A similar treatment is employed in the martagon lily border which also has turban flowers.

Tiger lily. Detail of the flower.

Tiger lily. The whole plant.

*Tiger lily. Stamped,
gold-plated plaque.*

*Tiger lily. Sprig-patterned
woven fabric. Straight match.*

41

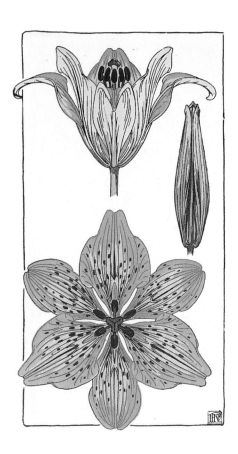

Saffron lily. Detail of the flower.

Opposite:
Stencilled sprig pattern.

SAFFRON AND MARTAGON LILIES

Verneuil's presentation of this saffron-coloured lily gave him the opportunity to demonstrate how from the same botanical inspiration one can proceed to very different ends: towards a simplification of the model or, alternatively, towards a more elaborate design. The different views of the flower are identical to those of the tiger lily except for the cup-shaped drawing, which the artist included here for the first time in this work. The dark tones of the floral-patterned stencil emphasize the pure elegance of this lily, even when it is flattened as if by a flower press. The sinuous lines of the foliage are the same as those used to draw the open flowers. Here, less becomes more. The design of the wallpaper border is in diametrical opposition to the spring pattern. The luxuriant foliage is abundant. In both cases there are three flowers per stem (two buds flanking an open blossom alternate with two open blossoms flanking a closed bud). The light blue flowers are surmounted by yellow pistils and stamens.

42

Martagon lily. Wallpaper border.

44

Saffron lily. Strip of appliqué fabrics.

FRITILLARY

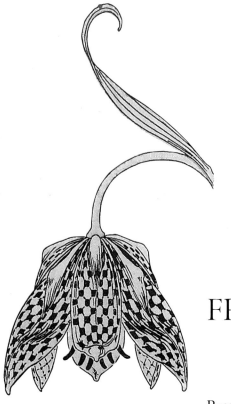

Better known nowadays as the chequered fritillary, *Fritillaria meleagris*, this little flower bulb is presented by Verneuil under the curious name of guinea fowl fritillary. Spring-blooming, the little bell-shaped flowers are covered by a regular check pattern in varying shades of purple. In a rather sombre botanical presentation, the designer featured its symmetry and characteristic habit. Several years later, in 1915, the Scottish architect and designer Charles Rennie Macintosh would interpret the same flower in soft, watercolour shades. His brother-in-law, an experienced amateur gardener, cultivated fritillaries which permitted Macintosh to study them in detail. In the two projects illustrated here, a wallpaper pattern and an embroidered border, Verneuil did not ostensibly modify the flowers, but the stems and foliage undergo a decorative transformation. First curving and arching them, he then twisted them in characteristic Art Nouveau arabesques. In fact, Macintosh's fritillary was very close to Verneuil's, drawn seven years earlier.

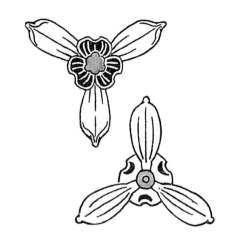

DAFFODIL AND SNOWDROP

Snowdrop. The whole plant and details of the flower.

Daffodil. Decorated plate.

The characteristic form of the pseudo-narcissus, or daffodil flower, lends itself to all types of stylization, as does the round-ended, fleshy foliage. Verneuil imagined a decorated plate with an asymmetrical design where two fully bloomed daffodils are surrounded by curved leaves. In the daffodil border the same foliage is rendered more gracefully. Repeating the same curved line from top to bottom and left to right, Verneuil then balanced the design by adding a single blade in the opposite direction. The two daffodil projects are closely related. In the triangular design the artist imposed strict symmetry. Abundant foliage originates from the middle of the base. The rigid blades are lined up, one next to the other, in two shades of green. The blade ends soften into strong arabesques. Verneuil's daffodils actually resemble his fuchsias. The rectangular design is quite similar, except that in this case the presentation is vertical. A delicate *chinoiserie*, the single-colour stencil is evidence of Verneuil's consummate graphic mastery. The pure, original lines transform the daffodil into an enchanted blossom.

The snowdrop, *Galanthus nivalus,* is an extremely well-known flower bulb, for its range as a wild flower extends from the Pyrenees to Asia. Its French name, *perce-neige*, originates from its winter flowering. The delicate green shoots literally push through the immaculate snow crust. The white, green-flecked flowers follow with their characteristic nod, as if bent under the weight of invisible snow. In the botanical study, oddly, the snowdrops become robust bulbs with thick-set stems. The scale the artist imposed is not nature's. The presentation is symmetrical, devoid of stylization or fantasy. In the black-ground, single-flower motif, Verneuil emphasized the characteristic drooping of the snowdrop.

From top to bottom:
Daffodil. Single-colour stencil.
Snowdrop. Border.
Daffodil. Border,

49

Daffodil.

Daffodil.

LADY'S-SLIPPER ORCHID

Cypripedium roezlii. *The whole plant and a detail of the flower.*

Opposite:
Cypripedium. Woven fabric.

Cypripedium roezlii adds an exotic note to a work largely dominated by more common European flora. Despite the rather coarse sounds of its botanical name, this orchid, or more exactly this genus of orchids, is better known by the name of lady's-slipper. Several species are indigenous to Europe. *Cypripedium* is composed of two Latin words: *Cypris* is one of the many names given to the goddess Venus and *pes* means foot. The species chosen by Verneuil is not one of the most common nowadays. His choice seems to have been motivated by the exaggerated length of the two side petals which twist in regular spirals before finishing with curled ends. The 'slipper' or labellum of the flower is the distinctive characteristic of the genus. In the leaded-glass project, while insisting on the symmetry of the foliage, Verneuil simplified the flower to the extreme. For a bookbinding, three flowers tilt forward menacingly, like octopuses stretching forth long, enveloping tentacles. An orchid plant with three flowers decorates the woven fabric. The ground is covered with fern leaves, most probably sprigs of fragile maidenhair.

Lady's-slipper orchid.
Leaded-glass window.

54

Lady's-slipper orchid.
Bookbinding.

55

ORCHIS

In *L'Etude de la plante et ses applications aux industries d'art,* Verneuil proposed two orchids. The second, the lady orchis, is also a ground orchid, a much less spectacular one than the lady's-slipper. Indigenous to Europe, the lady orchis is often found growing in fields in France. Its name is derived from the Greek: *orchis* means testicle, alluding to the tuberous roots of the plant. In his botanical study the artist included a view of the roots, perhaps to illustrate their connection with the plant name. It is one of the rare examples where Verneuil included a detail without exploiting it in the projects. Large, light-green leaves with distinctive length-wise ribs originate from the base. The orchis flower has two main colours: the labellum is light pink with touches of purple, while the upper petals, which form a hood, are darker with mixed shades of purple and black. Two stages of the flowering are depicted. In the beginning the inflorescence is a tight, oval spike; later, in full bloom, the florets become slack, and the inflorescence takes on a pyramidal shape. In the wallpaper project Verneuil alternates two different stages of flowering in two different sizes in a staggered arrangement.

Lady orchis. The whole plant.

Opposite:
Lady orchis. Wallpaper.

56

GARDEN FLOWERS

ANEMONES

Wood anemone. The whole plant and details of the flower.

Opposite:
Wood anemone. Embroidery.

Verneuil's botanical curiosity was piqued by two varieties of wild anemones. *Anemone nemorosa*, more commonly called wood anemone, grows on forest floors all over Europe and in the temperate regions of Asia. Its composite leaf, made up of three leaflets, dominates the botanical study. All around it, Verneuil arranged different views of the simple, white, six-petalled flower with numerous stamens. He imagined a plate decorated with three flowers and three leaves as if prepared for a herbal. Although the same flat presentation is utilized in the square-shaped design, the flowers and foliage are more stylized, surrounded by a white contour on a black background. Another anemone, the European pasque-flower, *Anemone pulsatilla*, is more elaborate. The delicate, fern-like foliage perfectly harmonizes with the large, single flower with its characteristic six petals and numerous stamens. The darker underside of the petals is silky. Once again Verneuil's talent is manifest in the embroidery project. Side and front views of the leaf are combined on a single stem. Flowers alternate with blow-balls. Above, the balls are blown apart as the seeds float about. In fact, Verneuil is illustrating the etymology of *anemone*. The word comes from the Greek *anemos*, wind, which sends the feathery anemone seeds flying.

60

Pasque-flower. Decorated plate.

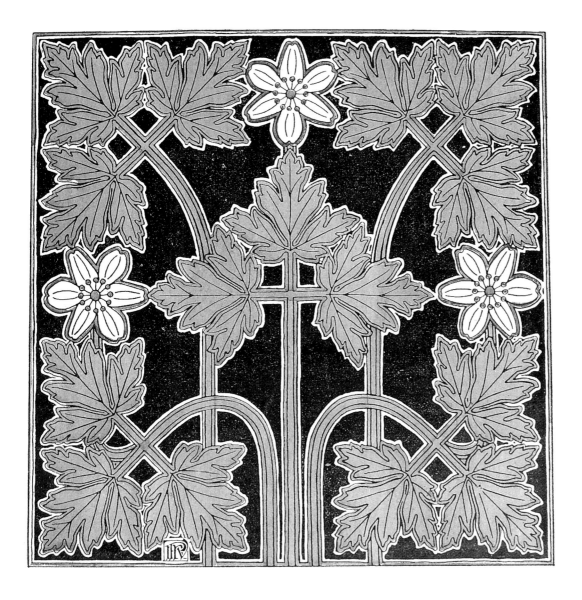

Pasque-flower. Decorated ground.

63

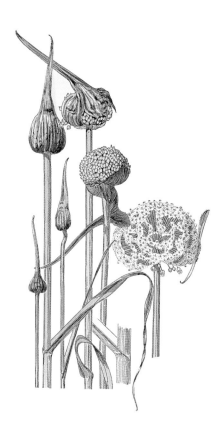

LEEK

Leek.
The whole plant and details
of the flower.

While Verneuil neglected garden vegetables somewhat, he could not help but be charmed by the elegance of the common leek. Classified among the *Allium*, which also include the onion and the garlic, the leek is no doubt the most decorative member of this large family. The strict, vertical architecture of the column-like stems is subdued by the soft, sinuous curves of the bluish-green leaves. In the botanical drawing, Verneuil demonstrated the aesthetic potential of the leek. Straight lines are opposed to the curves of the leaves as well as to the flower, which is shown undergoing the different stages of its development. Starting from a pear-shaped bulb at the end of the stem, the flower swells and rounds out before extracting itself from its sheath. Several times the pointed cap of the sheath breaks the line framing the drawing, as do the tips of the leaves which resemble unravelling ribbons. Exploited regularly by Verneuil in the *Study of the Plant*, this decorative mannerism exemplifies the artist's mastery of the visual aspects of drawing juxtaposed to words. In the introduction, he insisted upon the importance of adapting form to the space being decorated as well as to the material utilized. In the project he imagined for the leek, the artist went one step further. Not only did he adapt its height by giving preference to the upper part of the leaves and flowers, Verneuil also imagined the vegetable in a way which makes reference to its culinary use. He designed a soup tureen with a leek motif.

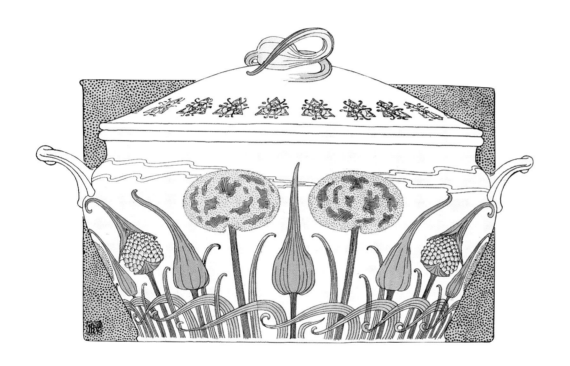

Leek. Soup tureen.

FUCHSIA

The whole plant and a detail of the flower.

Opposite:
Fuschia. Single-colour stencilled border.

The fuchsia reached Europe during the eighteenth century after having been discovered in San Domingo in the last years of the seventeenth century. The loud colours of its showy, even gaudy, flowers are what attracted Verneuil. The complex form lends itself easily to ornamentation. Often in contrasting colours, the petals extend from the tubular calyx which ends in four long sepals. The variety presented has strong red stems. In the botanical study of the fuchsia, the artist detailed the profile of the flower, emphasizing the different positions of the sepals which curl when fully open. The delicate petals emerge from them like crinolines from beneath a dress. The pollen-carrying stamens often protrude past the petals. In the presence of such a riot of colours, Verneuil's reaction was to use the fuchsia in a dark, understated design emphasizing its feminine delicacy. In the stencilled border, the artist exaggerated the serrated edges of the contorted leaves, while he lengthened the stamens to enhance the bell-shaped flowers.

CYCLAMEN

As a faithful observer of European flora, the artist could not overlook the cyclamen, which grows in cool underwoods. Every element of this plant is decorative, beginning with the foliage. While the large leaves are usually oval, they are also sometimes heart-shaped (Verneuil included both shapes). The edges are delicately notched. Crossing the dark green surface of the leaves, which are marked by irregularly shaped spots, the veins are lighter green. The flower is even more original. Held high above the foliage, it is composed of five erect petals, folded back and pointing upward. Seen from underneath, as Verneuil showed it well, it resembles a child's pinwheel. In both projects, the stained-glass border and the ceramic tile, the designer chose the same tones of yellow, green and brown, although actually no yellow variety of cyclamen exists. The flowers on the ceramic tile are in the pure Art Nouveau style: the leaf is presented flat, in a front view, while the flowers are presented in profile. The cyclamen in stained glass is similar to certain simplifications of the iris, a trilobate form, recalling the fleur-de-lis.

PRIMROSE

When Verneuil decided to include the primrose in *L'Etude de la plante et ses applications aux industries d'art*, his choice did not fall on the omnipresent cowslip primrose, *Primula veris*. Rather, his aesthetic eye was attracted by the more exotic Chinese primrose, *Primula sinensis*, introduced into Europe during the nineteenth century. Very little is known about its origin. In the botanical study the flowers are highlighted. Held above the foliage, they are grouped around the floral spike. In the same study Verneuil depicted different views of the flower, as well as the 'flower ball' seen from above which he rendered in simple lines. Seen from underneath, the leaf reveals its branching ribs. In the wallpaper pattern, the foliage steals the show from the yellow flowers. The artist tilts the plant towards the viewer, the leaves are arranged symmetrically around it, and behind the floral spike a leaf becomes a regal crown.

PERIWINKLE

The common periwinkle, *Vinca minor*, can be found on forest floors throughout Europe. This ground-cover plant has a tendency to colonize areas where it finds hospitable conditions. The artist preferred to figure it erect, its fragile stems climbing in search of light. The stem delicately advancing across the page from left to right illustrates the invasive nature of the plant. Minuscule roots are represented with the same lines as the foliage. Discreet, the clear blue flower blends into the green foliage. The coffee cup and saucer design were an opportunity for Verneuil to represent a flower on rounded surfaces. The garland of flowers and foliage encircling the saucer is in fact quite conventional. The other pattern is more striking because it emphasizes the swollen base of the cup. The four stages of a border represent a departure from the botanical plant. Here he preferred to highlight the foliage. They can be interpreted as a study in the relation between design and ground, and the most impressive is the simplest. The periwinkle is figured by a simple white contour against a dark ground.

Periwinkle. Coffee cup and saucer.

*Periwinkle. Embroidered
cushion.*

78

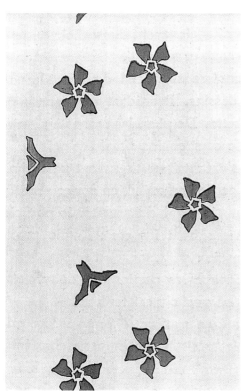

Periwinkle. Details of a three-colour border with reserve design.

79

GOURDS

Gourds and colocynths belong to the family of Cucurbitaceae, as do the pumpkin and the squash. They are the highly decorative members of a family dominated by edible vegetables. For all their elegant luxuriance they crawl along the ground next to the commonest of vegetables. Verneuil played this fact down, preferring to treat them as rare, exotic vines. For the colocynth the spherical gourds are marked by regular alternating sections of yellowy orange and dark green. The real interest of the design, however, resides in the treatment of the foliage and the tendrils. An oversized leaf dominates the botanical study, with lush greenery going off in all directions. Twisting and wrapping around each other, the tendrils epitomize the graphic exuberance of the Art Nouveau style. In the frieze Verneuil used this botanical detail to trace elegant arabesques. Departing from the botanical palette to colour the fruit a handsome dark blue on the painted glass, he played on the same aesthetic approach for the gourds.

Gourd. Detail of the fruit.

Gourd. Painted stained glass.

Colocynth. Detail of the fruit.

Colocynth. Frieze for a dining room.

WILD FLOWERS

TEASEL AND THISTLE

Rarely cultivated, the teasel is a tall plant, sometimes exceeding six or seven feet, which is indigenous to the Mediterranean region. It is often to be found growing along road embankments and in wastelands. Besides its botanical name, *Dipsacus fullonum*, it also has the more poetic common name of 'bird cabaret' in French, making reference to a particularity of the leaves. Opposite and joined at the stem, each pair of leaves forms a cup where it is intersected by the stem. Rainwater collects there, and small insects fall in and drown. Hungry birds congregate there to drink and eat. In fact, the botanical name is derived from two Greek words meaning 'to cure thirst'. Obviously the birds are not the only ones to exploit this oasis. In the botanical study Verneuil accentuated this foliage characteristic as he did the prickles lining the stems. However, what seems to have held his attention the most was the complex architecture of the inflorescence. Arranged around the large receptacle which is covered with pointed egrets, tiny florets bloom layer by layer. In the sprig pattern the botanical model is only slightly modified; two quite similar motifs alternate in staggered position. By inventing his own hybrid teasel, Verneuil departed from scientific precision in the stained-glass border. The flowers here resemble two-tone insects with carefully folded wings.

The thistle is a plant especially cherished by Art Nouveau artists and designers. Its characteristic silhouette was often utilized in glassware, marquetry and wrought iron. Verneuil adopted *Silybum Marianum*, the St Mary thistle, which is similar to teasel. Both are tall, thorny plants with complex architecture. Also indigenous to the Mediterranean region, the St Mary thistle adds interest in the garden with its foliage as well as its flowers, which are a favourite for dried arrangements. Certain gardeners eliminate the flowers in order to stimulate the growth of impressive clumps of untouchable leaves. The thistle inspired two projects – but no botanical study – in which Verneuil gave full rein to a side of his design talent he rarely showed in his work. Both are elaborate, highly intricate patterns. Composed of a single, large motif, the woven fabric design is very extravagant. The staggered positioning is so compact that it is quite difficult to delimit the basic motif. The lace project is just as atypical and elaborate. Flowers in various stages of blooming alternate with several leaf shapes. The light-coloured ribbing of the leaves provides vertical references which facilitate the deciphering of the design.

Teasel. The whole plant and a detail of the flower.

Opposite:
Teasel. Sprig pattern paper.

86

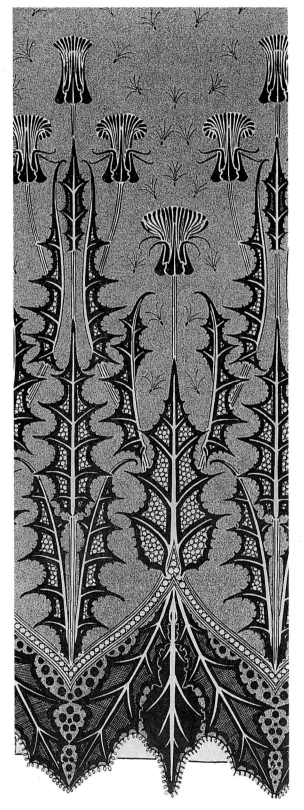

Left:
Teasel. Stained-glass window.
Right:
Thistle. Lace.

Opposite:
Thistle. Woven fabric.

DANDELION

As with the thistle, Verneuil chose not to include a botanical study of the dandelion. Two projects are proposed: a fan and a bookbinding. In the first case, the shape of the motif is dictated by that of the object. Leaves and blow-balls alternate around the fan. The flat, serrated-edge leaves are composed of a series of overlapping triangles diminishing in size from top to bottom. Resembling exotic trees or totem poles, their jagged shape also reminds one that dandelion comes from the French 'lion tooth'. The blow-ball is carried on a rigid stem between two small leaves, similar to the larger ones. Light-coloured circles contrast with the darker leaves. Verneuil's bookbinding project is a superb example of his artistic virtuosity. A simple line rendering of a large dandelion plant is placed at the bottom centre. The irregular outline of the leaf is faithfully represented. Two types of blow-balls are figured, one complete, the other a simple 'halo' of seeds. The roundness of the balls corresponds perfectly to the curves of the leaves. Around the edge of the cover, two types of blow-balls alternate, while in the centre, completing the design, is a staggered sprig pattern of individual seeds.

Dandelion. Lace fan.

Dandelion. Gilding. Punch and fillet.

COLUMBINE

Columbine. The whole plant and detail of the flower.

As with the fuchsia and the cyclamen, the elaborate architecture of the columbine flower is captivating. It is not at all surprising that Verneuil was enthused by its decorative potential. Groups or single specimens of five-petalled flowers hang downward from the end of delicate stems. At the base of the flower is a spur which prolongs it. This detail inspired its botanical name, *Aquilegia*, which is derived from the latin *aquila*, meaning eagle. The reference is most probably to the curved claws of this bird of prey. The length and exact shape of the spur determine the different varieties of columbine. Three projects are presented, a woven fabric and two decorative grounds, one of which is produced by a single-colour stencil. The columbine motif used on the fabric is faithful to the botanical plant. Three identical flowers fan out above the foliage. The flower and leaf on the matching border are more stylized. On the decorative ground the flat tints of the leaf contrast with the delicate flower. The flower on the stencil is very close to certain fuchsia designs.

Columbine. Woven fabric.

*Columbine. Ornamental
ground.*

*Opposite:
Columbine. Single-colour
stencil.*

94

FOXGLOVE

Foxglove. The whole plant and a detail of the flower.

A medicine well known for its beneficial effect on the heart, digitalis is extracted from a tall perennial which easily reaches three feet in height. By illustrating *Digitalis purpurea*, Verneuil chose one of the most common garden varieties and exactly the one used by the pharmaceutical industry. To accentuate the height of the plant, the artist figured it in two parts, the bottom separated from the top, an accepted convention in botanical illustration. Thus, he could detail the voluminous leaves around the base of the solid stalk, in much the same way as he represented the impressive floral spike. The flower with its long, tubular purple corolla is illustrated in various views; the inside is covered with large, deep-red spots surrounded in white against a ground of smaller dots. The lower lip is lined with fine hairs. The florets are carried close to the spike, the corolla opening towards the bottom. In the ceramic tile project, the floral motif is complete in three vertical tiles; at the base of the plants, a heart-shaped leaf links the motifs horizontally. The florets in the vertical axis are coloured in darker tones than the surrounding ones, thus accentuating the verticality of the design.

Foxglove. Wainscoting.

97

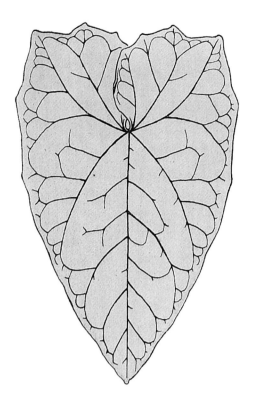

BINDWEED

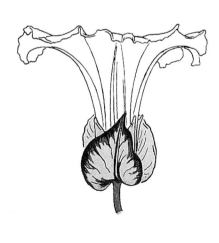

Bindweed. Details of the plant.

Should the fact that Verneuil included not one but two botanical studies of a plant which is universally regarded as the gardener's bane be considered aesthetic provocation? Hedge glorybind, also known by the botanical name *Calystegia sepium*, is an extremely vigorous climbing plant. In the space of a few weeks, the vine is capable of enveloping all the supports and plants that happen to be in its path, smothering them under luxuriant heart-shaped foliage. Once again it was the blooming process that fascinated Verneuil. Chronicling the unfolding of the flower in a series of botanically accurate renderings, he compressed a timespan of several days into the two pages of his scientific studies. As an observant spectator of detail, the artist invited those who would use his work to follow his example: inspect and study plants without preconceived ideas. Thanks to his talent, all plants – be they lowly, even bothersome, weeds or the stately iris or lily – are suitable for decorative patterning. In the second study, the glorybind wraps itself around the victim plant in much the same manner as the design envelops the page. For a lace collar Verneuil exploited the leaf form and the twining stems to produce delicate arabesques. In another project the invasive stem and tender yellow blossoms encircle a cylindrical vase.

Bindweed. Lace collar.

Hedge glorybind.

Bindweed. Vase.

LILY OF THE VALLEY

Lily of the valley. The whole plant and detail of the leaf.

Opposite:
Lily of the valley. Wallpaper.

A work on the ornamental applications of plants would be incomplete if it overlooked the lily of the valley. The small, bell-shaped florets often decorated turn-of-the-century glassware and porcelain. In France this plant engendered an industry built around the coincidence of its flowering with the Labour Day celebration on 1 May. In honour of the plant, Verneuil produced a botanical study and two projects, a wallpaper pattern and a vase. The study is rather dry, of no great interest in fact. It is a rather simple inventory of the different aspects of the plant without stylization or decorative repetition. The smooth, oval leaves lined with length-wise ribbing originate from the base of the plant, and the characteristic bell-shaped, fragrant white flowers all hang to the same side of the floral spike. The wallpaper pattern is an excellent opportunity for the designer to produce a dense, sophisticated composition in green and white.

102

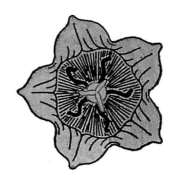

BELLFLOWER OR CAMPANULA

Among the numerous varieties of bellflowers, Verneuil's preference went to *Campanula rotundifolia*, one of the simpler. The plant has two distinct leaf forms. Rounded, almost heart-shaped, the first leaves, which die off later when the plant flowers, are faithfully represented at the base of the bellflower in the botanical study. The leaves of the adult plant are narrow and linear, the bell-shaped flowers bluish-violet. In the project of a shaped cylindrical vase, Verneuil presented all the above-mentioned details. In fact, the botanical study was simply transposed on to the vase, a form which, furthermore, was particularly easy to decorate. For an unpretentious flower the artist proposed a simple presentation with little stylization.

Bellflower. The whole plant and a detail of the flower.

Bellflower. Vase.

HORN POPPY

Horn poppy. The whole plant and a detail of the flower.

Horn poppies are native to southern Europe and especially to the countries bordering the Mediterranean Sea. Verneuil most probably chose to represent *Glaucium flavum*. As its common name suggests, the blooming of the flower is very similar to that of true poppies. As an attentive nature lover, Verneuil never grew tired of chronicling step after step the days and hours leading up to the blossoming of the flowers. The basal leaves have deeply irregular indentations, quite similar to dandelion leaves. With his usual minute detailing, Verneuil also figured the oddly shaped leaves growing further up the stem. The blue-green colour of the foliage also plays its part (in Greek, *glaukion* means 'bluish plant'). In comparison, the colour of the flowers is a much brighter, franker yellow. Composed of four petals, they are arranged in a funnel-like shape. What probably interested Verneuil particularly in the horned poppy was the smooth, curved seed capsule, which is often a foot long. In the border the plant is illustrated from the side; the flower is encircled by an arched ring reminiscent of the shape of the seed capsule.

Horn poppy. Border.

BITTER NIGHTSHADE

Bitter nightshade, or *Solanum dulcamara,* is a climbing bush. The composite leaves are oval and somewhat heart-shaped at the base. Held above the foliage, the abundant white flowers are arranged in cymes; their corollas are delicately rolled petals. The toxic red berries are quite similar in shape to the flowers. For a black background embroidered cushion, Verneuil placed the supple stems in the four corners, reserving the centre for four bunches of white blossoms. The stems end in partially opened leaves which form stylized arabesques around them. The linear presentation of the frieze is finer, lighter, but in the end the two interpretations are not that different. In the latter, berries are substituted for flowers and the leaf renderings are simple lines.

108

Bitter Nightshade.
Embroidered cushion.

MISTLETOE

This plant often inspired artists and craftsmen at the turn of the century. In 1894, the Daum crystalworks at Nancy, France, produced 'Au Gui l'an neuf', a high-necked vase with shaped base – a pure Art Nouveau creation of decorative glass. Its clear and bright green frosted glass was ornamented with sprigs of mistletoe. At the same time the Sèvres porcelain factory created a small vase decorated with blue and yellow mistletoe. And at the beginning of the present century the Lunéville china factory in eastern France brought out their tea and coffee set famous for its shaped pieces where the dishevelled aspect of the plant is largely accentuated. In the two examples of leaded glass here, Verneuil imagined the plant from a different angle and preferred to emphasize its strict geometry. The plant form is pressed as it would be on the page of a herbal and then repeated, the fine lines of lead linking the different parts. For the wrought-iron fence, he succeeded in giving the same impression of lightness by repeating a simple pair of mistletoe leaves; the bunches of berries seem to have been borrowed from his ivy designs. Showing once again his consummate talent for layout, Verneuil repeated the pair of leaves in the two stencilled borders.

Mistletoe. The whole plant.

Mistletoe. Single-colour stencilled border.

Mistletoe. Leaded-glass.

Mistletoe. Wrought-iron fence.

IVY

Opposite:
Ivy. Inlaid wood ground.

Verneuil created four projects for ivy: a wrought-iron hinge and escutcheon, a point lace curtain and an inlaid wood design. The latter is composed of oversized five-lobed leaves interconnected with bunches of berries. Of the same style, the hinge and escutcheon were most probably meant to be placed on the same support. Of equal importance here, foliage and fruit alternate around the hinge shaft. Asymmetrical, the ribbings in the three different leaf models are composed of intricate fine lines. On the escutcheon the intertwining stems finishing in a single, asymmetrical swirl around the keyhole summarize the Art Nouveau style. Strangely enough, Verneuil chose to ignore the major characteristic of this plant. As everyone knows, ivy is a tenacious climber, capable of dislodging apparently solid walls. The designer, however, tamed it to represent dainty ivy sprigs on the lace curtain, once again accentuating the stylized leaf ribbing.

Ivy. Point lace curtain.

116

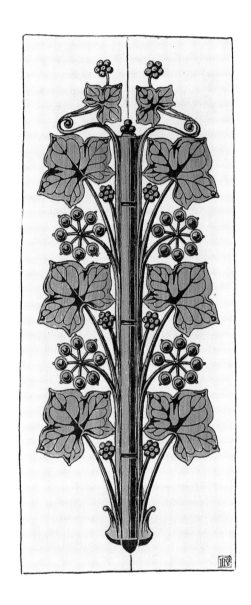

Ivy. Wrought-iron hinge.
Wrought-iron escutcheon.

117

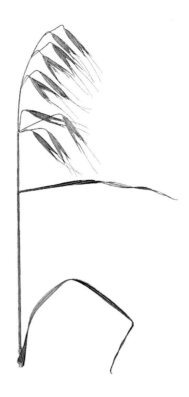

OATS

Oats, like wheat, belong to the important family of Graminaceae, which can be divided into two major groups: edible grains and decorative grasses. Both have characteristic inflorescences with drooping spikes. Some are feathery, others are even more wispy, agitated by the slightest puff of air. Cereals were often sources of inspiration for Verneuil and his contemporaries: designs of wheat, oats and others were mixed without distinction. On Gallé plates and Daum decorative glass they are presented with field poppies, the transparency of glass accentuating the lightness of the plant forms. In the botanical study Verneuil allowed himself a great liberty of presentation. A long, narrow leaf crosses the page, dividing it in half. He continued in like fashion in the woven fabric project: there the artistic gesture is completely liberated. Composed of an extravagant, wind-shaken inflorescence with an elegant figure-eight stem on a sprig-patterned ground, the design can be likened to sophisticated calligraphy.

CORN

Corn. Details of the cob and bracts.

Like the leek, corn represents one of the rare inroads into edible vegetables in *L'Etude de la plante*. *Zea mays*, its botanical name, has been cultivated in central America for at least five millennia. Oddly enough, however, corn is not to be found in a wild state. A mature plant can easily reach the impressive height of six to twelve feet. By only drawing a small section of the stalk, Verneuil avoided the scale problems that the representation of the whole plant would have entailed. This small part of the whole was also the basis of a fabric design. In the botanical study the solid stalk is placed vertically, while the cylindrical cob with its compact rows of pea-sized kernels is held almost horizontally. But apparently neither the cob nor the yellowish-green kernels captured Verneuil's eye. His interest was concentrated on the abundant bracts surrounding and protecting the cob. Their number seems to be a gross exaggeration, but a conscious one, because he took great care to twist and bend them, rumpling them in the same way he would highly sophisticated drapery. In the project of an embroidered fabric with appliqués, the plant is simplified, the bracts eliminated from the cob. The vertical motif is repeated along an endless stalk. A single sheath unfurls, like a long streamer waving around the stalk.

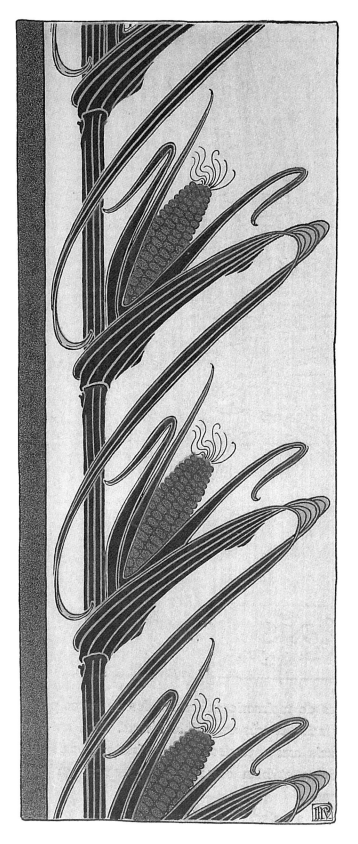

Corn. Embroidered fabric with appliqués.

123

AQUATIC PLANTS

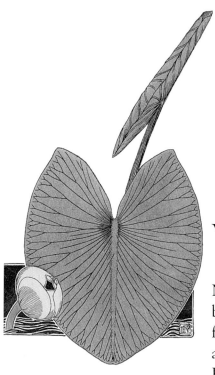

WATER LILY

Nenuphars, more commonly known as water lilies, are all members of the same botanical family, the Nymphaeaceae. In his treatment Verneuil showed no favouritism toward the white water lily, the best-known member of the family, and gave equal importance to the European cow lily, *nufar luteum*. Furthermore, if the botanical studies differ in their layout, they both emphasize the same aspects of the two plants. The blooming flower is represented next to the dominant element of the composition, a very large, flat leaf. Smaller and more compact, the yellow flower of the cow lily resembles that of the buttercup; it is much less spectacular than that of the white varieties. The border composition is more complex than it would seem. A slightly staggered line of small, closed flowers occupies the upper half, which is counterbalanced by a repetition of larger, fully bloomed ones in the bottom half. Surrounding them are large, flat, heart-shaped leaves. A muted green seed receptacle occupies the centre of the larger flowers. Representing the aquatic setting of the plants, sinuous, dark-blue lines animate the background. The decorated ground combines a yellow flower whose shape resembles that of the white water lily with an elongated leaf very close to that of the cow lily.

When Verneuil published *L'Etude de la plante* in 1908, water lilies were very much the craze. A Frenchman was partially responsible. A nurseryman located in the Lot et Garonne, Latour Marliac, obtained a hybrid which he multiplied and commercialized around the world. Claude Monet, an accomplished gardener, installed a large pond on his property in Giverny to cultivate aquatic plants, before immortalizing them in a group of monumental paintings. White water lilies benefit from the exotic imagery of the lotus, linking them with the Orient and ancient Egypt. In the botanical study, Verneuil once again followed the flower from the stage of a tightly closed bud to the mature flower. The oversized leaf in the foreground copies the presentation used for the colocynth. The pavement design plays on the difference between the size of the leaf and the flower. The small flower is small and squared, the generous leaf curvilinear.

Cow lily. Detail of the plant.

Cow lily. Ornamental ground.

127

Cow lily. Border.

128

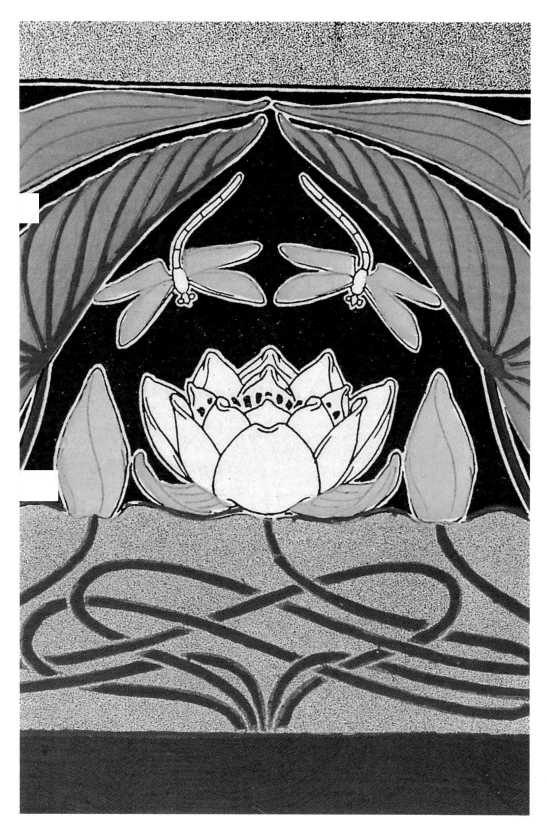

Water lily and arrowhead.
Wallpaper border.

Following pages:
Water lily. Detail of the plant.
Water lily. Pavement.

129

SEAWEED

Free as a bird, or perhaps one should say, free as seaweed. Seaweed is the common name given to a wide variety of aquatic plants. One of the easiest ways of defining them is by all the basic structures they lack: stems, leaves and roots. Their unique qualities have led artists and designers to interpret them in very fanciful ways. Consequently, Verneuil presented no botanical representation, preferring only to propose projects. In the oceans throughout the world, many types of seaweed exist, some very extravagant; Verneuil, however, limited his use to the most identifiable of these aquatic plant forms. The artist figured the seaweed as long ribbons with scalloped edges, voluptuously undulating at the mercy of the sea currents. In both the background of the painted glass project and the blue-green border, round air bubbles rise, contrasting with long, linear plant shapes. In the same way that he did for the leek-patterned soup tureen, the designer imagined a perfect equation between the plant and the object. The waving curves of the blue seaweed correspond perfectly to the rounded base of a water pitcher and matching basin.

Seaweed. Border.

Seaweed. Water pitcher and matching basin.

133

Seaweed. Detail of a border.

Opposite:
Seaweed. Painted glass.

134

ARROWHEAD

The arrowhead is a decorative aquatic or marsh plant often cultivated along pond banks. Some varieties, notably *Sagittaria sagittifolia*, are indigenous to Europe, although most come from the temperate and tropical zones of the Americas. Verneuil's drawing seems to be of *Sagittaria obtusa*. Its outstanding feature is the very large leaf – up to eight inches long – which is easily identifiable by its characteristic oval shape and its two rounded lobes coming to a point. The central ribbing exaggerates its size. In Verneuil's own words, the colour is 'cool green', while the underside is a much darker shade. Very similar to those of the peach, the small, pinkish-white flowers are arranged around a solid floral spike. This resemblance brought about the common name of 'water peach' for the arrowhead. The oblique border is interesting for several reasons, the first and most obvious being the very fact that it is oblique, which gave the artist the opportunity to solve a specific design problem. Verneuil took advantage of the possibilities of a triangular leaf and loaded the plant with abundant blossoms. The general treatment of the patterns foreshadows the decorative style that followed Art Nouveau, Art Deco.

Arrowhead. The whole plant.

136

Arrowhead. Oblique border.

CATTAIL

The characteristic form of the thick cylindrical spikes makes this plant easily identifiable. Its botanical name, *Typha*, is attributed to Theophrastus. Six species with different origins populate European marshlands. Although now they are often connected with the most conventional dried floral arrangements, their past was more illustrious. In times of famine, the farinaceous rhizomes were consumed, while other varieties were used to make paper. Decidedly elegant, the plant is none the less limited to some extent as a decorative element because it is so vertical. Originating from the base, the leaves are extremely long and linear, bending naturally under their own weight. Verneuil imagined a tall, leaded-glass window using a cattail design. The leaves stretch and curve like docile ribbons. The same sinuous curves are repeated in the blue water. The heavy spikes are somewhat lost among the wavy leaves. The fine bars of lead gracefully break up the imposing verticality.

Cattail. The whole plant and detail.

138

Cattail. Coloured glass window.

139

LEAVES AND TREES

Simple leaves

LEAVES

In *L'Etude de la plante et ses applications aux industries d'art,* the plant world provided Verneuil with an almost inexhaustible store of decorative motifs. In this respect the leaf is of prime importance: it inspired the artist as much as or more so than the flower. As an often symmetrical plane surface, the leaf is by definition a motif in itself. Be it the leaf of tiny plants or mighty trees, of clover or hazel, of periwinkle or acacia (these are Verneuil's examples), it simply has to be repeated and set out on a ground. The regular and irregular sprig patterns are two cases in point. Curiously enough, the leaf form has been reworked. It seems in fact to be a cross between an oak leaf and a bird feather. In the two leaded-glass projects, the same leaf motif appears quite different due to subtle modifications of tone combinations and the positioning of the lead connectors.

Ornamental leaf grounds.

Following pages:
Oak leaves. Regular and
irregular sprig patterns.

143

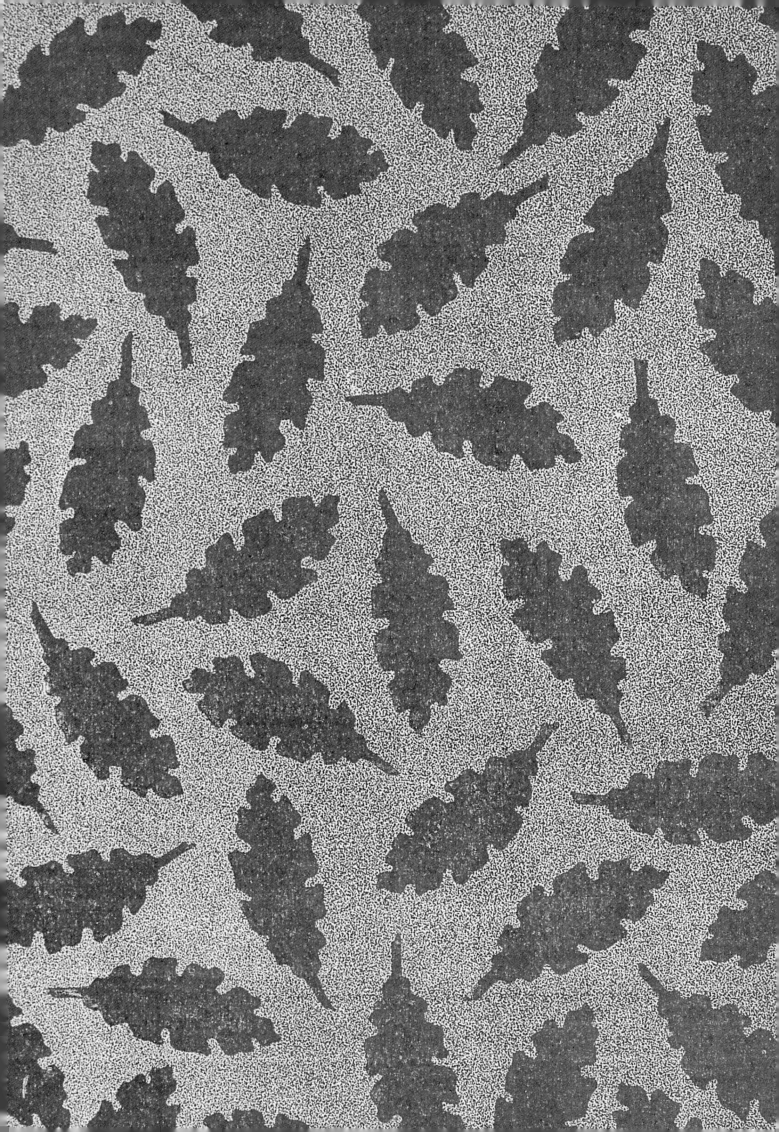

Leaves. Leaded glass.

Leaves. Leaded glass.

OAK AND HAZEL

Hazel. Border.

Opposite:
Oak. Ornamental ground.

Revered throughout ancient Europe, the oak was a sacred tree invested with powers from a supreme divinity. Symbol of strength, power and might (it attracted lightning), this majestic tree had exceptional status. In comparison, the hazel is much more modest. Shooting up rapidly, this bush or small tree is most sociable, and is often found growing in hedgerows surrounded by all types of plants and shrubs. Its botanic name, *Corylus*, meaning hood or helmet, makes reference to the fancy husk around the hazelnuts. Verneuil found a common denominator in the fruit of these two trees, acorns and hazelnuts. The acorn is elongated, while the cup at its base, which is actually made of overlapping scales, has been simplified here and is decorated with small blue spots. The bunches of olive-green leaves contrast with the bright yellow acorns. The hazelnut border is pure delight, as much for the bountiful size of the nuts as for the fanciful, lace-like, reddish-yellow husks surrounding them.

CHESTNUT

Chestnut. Bronze coping.

Opposite:
*Chestnut. Single-colour
stencilled ornamental ground.*

What would spring be without the spectacular flowering of the chestnut trees? Those gaudy bunches of flowers grouped in terminal panicles are a sure sign nature has once again come alive. They bring to mind baroque candelabras or tiered wedding cakes. Verneuil, however, ignored them completely and concentrated on the composite leaf and the prickly nut cases. On the single-colour stencilled ornamental ground, the leaves and nuts are set in a rhombus-shaped motif. Three leaves are surmounted by a bunch of spiny cases. In the bronze coping, the round pods connect the leaflets of the fan-shaped leaves. The surrounding motif is a slightly modified version of the ornamental ground motif.

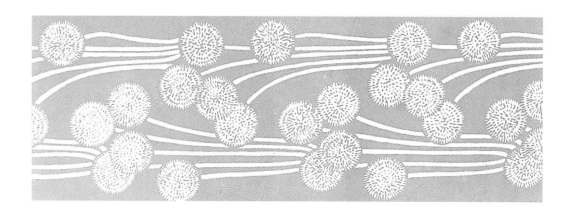

PLANE

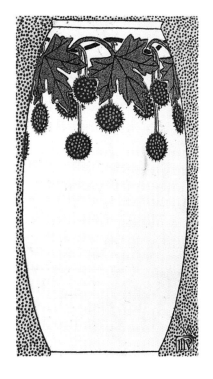

Plane. Border.
Plane. Vase.

Opposite:
Plane.
Detail of an inlaid wood border.

The plane is a most stately tree. Its Latin name, *Platanus*, derived from the Greek *platus*, meaning flat and large, makes reference to the leaf shape. In the black-ground inlaid wood frieze, Verneuil placed dark-green leaves with accentuated light ribbing of the same colour as the numerous seed balls. Branch ends bend in elegant but solid arabesques. The seeds – achenes held together by tufts of down in solid balls – hang behind the leaves. If the artist remained faithful to the botanical details of the tree in the border and the frieze, the design of the tall, shaped cylindrical vase is a departure from nature. Through slight line modifications he succeeded in transforming the plane leaves and balls into graceful grape vines. The twining, curved stems wrap around the vase neck, while the large, lobed plane leaf has been metamorphosed into a grape leaf. The staggered seed balls hang slackly. In the border design, balls which seem to be from the plane tree hang from extremely long stems. Verneuil has most certainly invented a new tree.

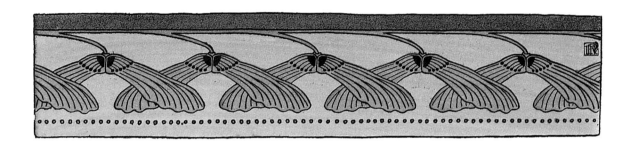

MAPLE

Maple. Inlaid gilt leather belt.

Opposite:
Maple. Tiles.

From one of the maples, the sycamore, Verneuil has created two design projects – a ceramic tile and a leather belt – finding inspiration in the rather discreet seeds of this tree. The achenes have two wings which allow them to 'fly', descending to the ground in a twisting spiral movement. The technical name for this winged seed is samara. On the inlaid gilt leather belt, the design is most simple. The winged seeds overlap, one wing in front, the other behind; they are counterbalanced by a line of small dots underneath. On the tile the artist combined seeds and leaves. The dark-green leaves contrast with the yellow diamond shapes formed by two samaras.

WISTERIA

Wisteria is a climbing shrub. Over the years its powerful branches encircle any supports found along the way. As it progresses, even wrought-iron fences must give way. Here, however, the plant is synonymous with lightness. The foliage – composite leaves with eleven or thirteen leaflets according to Verneuil – is given precedence over the flowers: only one bunch has blossomed. In the botanical study the artist created depth by varying the various green tones and the positions of the foliage. On one side the branch ends pass beyond the frame, a stylistic mannerism so dear to the artist, while on the other side the foliage is constrained by the frame. In the border a feeling of depth is achieved by superimposing two motifs one on top of the other. The leaves are arranged in loose spirals, while a bunch of flowers is delicately placed in the centre. The leaf ends disappear behind the limits of the design.

Wisteria. Border.

157

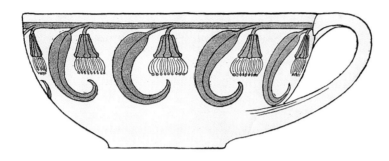

EUCALYPTUS

The eucalyptus foliage undergoes a rather complex evolution. The shape of the leaves changes several times before reaching the definitive one of the adult leaf. Thus, on the same tree, leaves of varying shapes and sizes are to be found. Verneuil preferred to simplify matters by representing only one type of leaf, the one most often connected with the tree. He depicted a simple, elongated leaf with a curved end, very similar to the one he drew for mimosa. In both projects he reminds us that eucalyptus is a highly decorative tree with showy flowers. The abundant red stamens are the most visible aspect of the flowers. They resemble delicate powder puffs attached to the boughs. On the black-ground fabric with appliqués and embroidery, the discreet arabesques of the leaves stand out from the rounded curves of the flowers by a subtle play on varying tones of dark blue. Considering the medicinal properties of eucalyptus, the tisane cup is very appropriate. One flower and one leaf alternate around the cup connected to an endless, ribbon-like stem.

Eucalyptus. Tisane cup.

Eucalyptus. Embroidered fabric with appliqués.

159

JASMINE

Indigenous to Iran, China, northern India and the Caucasus, white jasmine, or *Jasminum officinale*, is a climbing shrub with numerous healing properties. A sedative, it can soothe a cough and is also effective against headaches. A Chinese variety is used to flavour tea. White jasmine can grow to a height of sixteen to twenty-two feet. The opposite leaves are composed of seven oval leaflets; the thin boughs are shiny green. Very fragrant, the white flowers with four petals are grouped in small bunches at the bough ends. Seen from above, the four petals form a cross. In very muted tones of green, the botanical study is very close to that of wisteria, though unfortunately without the latter's graphic force or elegance. By its refined selection of tints, the vertical border is as strikingly exotic as the study is discreet and restrained. Verneuil remodelled the leaf shape by considerably elongating the top leaflet. The golden yellow flowers fan out on a dark ground. Very appropriately the designer imagined jasmine in the role of a captivating tropical flower.

Jasmine. The whole plant.

Jasmine. Vertical border.

MIMOSA

Mimosa calls to mind a picture of fragrant, diaphanous, bright yellow flowers, like small tufts of wool. They bloom at a time of the year when fresh flowers are scarce. Actually, what is often called mimosa does not belong to the botanical genus *Mimosa*; the 'sensitive plant', however, *Mimosa pudica*, is a true mimosa. Our plant is an acacia indigenous to Australia, introduced in France during the nineteenth century. With neither fantasy nor exuberance, the botanical study is faithful and straightforward. The foliage of Verneuil's mimosa is quite different from that of the recent popular varieties. Instead of the delicate composite leaf, this one quite resembles the long, curved, dark-green leaf of the eucalyptus. The pattern is practically identical in the border and the stencilled sprig pattern. The motif of the latter depicts simple round flowers lining the gently curving stems drawn in one sure stroke. With more generously arching curves and more abundant foliage, the lines of the border repeat those of the sprig pattern.

APPENDIX

APPENDIX
ORNAMENTAL GROUNDS

Maurice Pillard Verneuil
Extract from L'Etude de la plante et ses applications aux industries d'art.

Ornamental grounds decorate a whole surface, either by one or more repeating motifs, or by motifs in a sprig pattern where the only concern is balance. In the first case, the ornamental ground is called by the more specific name of repetitive ground; in the second case, it is called a sprig pattern.

But let us first define the role of the ornamental ground.

A surface cannot or must not accommodate a prominent ornamental motif. However, we do not want to leave it bare. What should be used? An ornamental ground.

Here is another example. Ornamental motifs decorate a surface. Between the motifs the ground is most often visible. So how do we enrich the ornamentation, create a link between the motifs, or embellish the ground with secondary, less conspicuous motifs? Once again, with an ornamental ground.

What types of ornamentation can decorate this ground? All types, provided that they are done well: geometrical, ornaments, flowers, foliage, animals. We will only concern ourselves with plant ornamental grounds, since that is the scope of this study. To construct them we shall be obliged, however, to concern ourselves with geometrical repetitive grounds.

Repetitive grounds, and for that matter ornamental grounds, are not a recent invention. Throughout time, various civilizations have utilized them in varying degrees. Some civilizations were especially active in the task. The Egyptians passed very interesting ones on to us, simple combinations most frequently based on geometrical patterns. The Japanese and the Arabs were decidedly past masters in this art form.

Arabic art provides innumerable accomplished examples of geometrical grounds executed in sculpture and even in painting, as well as in pavements, wood panelling and marquetry. Interlacing was pushed to its final limits. The decorators' ingenuity was consummate and the effects created were especially powerful.

As for Japanese monumental art, great efforts were made to diversify ornamental grounds, be they geometrical or not. They used birds in flight, foliage, flowers, or purely linear figures composed of squares, rhombuses, etc. But in most cases the geometrical repetitive ground is implemented for the ordering of motifs, or to delimit the surfaces to be decorated.

We have given several examples of Japanese or Moorish repetitive grounds here and explained their geometrical construction. These examples are obviously quite simple. But in Arabic art, the construction can become very complicated. Among the Japanese examples, the first three are based on the square. The hexagon and the equilateral triangle constitute the substructures of the following ones. For the last two, a rhombus with either simple or enhanced sides is the basic building block.

In like manner, in the Moorish repetitive grounds the square has been stood on one of its angles or one of its bases, and the hexagon and the equilateral triangle are utilized as construction lines.

But how shall we treat these geometrical repetitive grounds if our only concern here is plant forms? In the same way that the grid based on the triangle, the square, or any other figure helps us to build our repetitive ground, the repetitive ground will help us to build the ornamental ground.

A plant form—a whole plant, a flower or a leaf—must be inscribed in each of the elements. This is where we must find an ingenious interpretation of the chosen plant form in respect to its designated space...

This ground is based on the square. Another one of daffodils and foliage utilizes the equilateral triangle and the hexagon. This repetitive ground is based on the triangle and the rhombus.

As can be seen in the examples, ornamental grounds constitute an endless array of resources for the decorator. The geometrical combinations are infinite; on the same plotting, different plants can provide quite different ornamental grounds.

We have only indicated several very simple constructions based on elemental figures. Everyone will be able to find other combinations of lines and surfaces to compose appealing repetitive grounds with the pentagon, the octagon or still other geometrical figures as the basic element.

To these repetitive grounds must be added regular and irregular sprig patterns, although they are considerably different. While the interest of repetitive grounds lies exclusively in the fact that their elements stress their intentionally geometrical construction, even more so since they are highly compressed one against the other, sprig patterns, composed of identical or assorted elements, are less restrained, lighter. They are dispersed over the decorated surface, according to a large-scale plotting; or even in a completely irregular manner with no other criterion but adequate effect. We shall pay particular attention to a faultless balance of the motifs, so that the decorated surface presents a homogeneous appearance, without empty or overly charged spaces.

We have given two examples of oak leaf sprig patterns, the first regular, the second irregular. The regular pattern is more formal, the irregular one is freer, more unpredictable. It goes without saying, however, that the second example will have in certain cases only a semblance of irregularity. On a wallpaper or a fabric, the sprig pattern will be irregular on the initial repeat, but afterwards, it will be duplicated regularly over the entire surface. However, the general appearance will be even more informal, depending on how conspicuous the repetition is, and how many motifs are printed on each repeat.

Even more so for sprig patterns than for ornamental grounds, the diversity is infinite and our imagination can invent innumerable examples.

BIBLIOGRAPHY

Works by Maurice Pillard Verneuil:

L'Animal dans la décoration, Paris, 1898.
L'Ornementation par le pochoir, Paris, 1898.
Combinaisons ornementales se multipliant à l'infini à l'aide du miroir, Paris, 1901
(in collaboration with Georges Auriol and Alphonse Mucha).
Deux-cent-cinquante bordures, Paris, 1904.
Etude de la plante et ses applications aux industries d'art, Paris, 1908.
Etoffes japonaises tissées et brochées, Paris, 1910.
Etudes de la mer, Paris, 1913.